CANDLEWICK PRESS

Text copyright © 2022 by Martin Jenkins. Illustrations copyright © 2022 by Jane McGuinness. All rights reserved. No part of this book may be reproduced, transmitted, or stored in an information retrieval system in any form or by any means, graphic, electronic, or mechanical, including photocopying, taping, and recording, without prior written permission from the publisher. First US edition 2024. Library of Congress Catalog Card Number pending. ISBN 978-1-5362-3404-6. This book was typeset in HVD Bodedo and Hammersmith One. The illustrations were done in mixed media. Candlewick Press, 99 Dover Street, Somerville, Massachusetts 02144. www.candlewick.com.
Printed in Shenzhen, Guangdong, China. 24 25 26 27 28 29 CCP 10 9 8 7 6 5 4 3 2 1

FIND OUT ABOUT
Animal Tools

Martin Jenkins

illustrated by
Jane McGuinness

Tools are really useful—they help humans make stuff and move things around. Some other animals also use tools, often made from sticks, stones, and grass. Animals use tools mostly to get food, and sometimes they use them in surprising ways—here are some . . .

This animal sews leaves for its nest—
it does a very neat job!

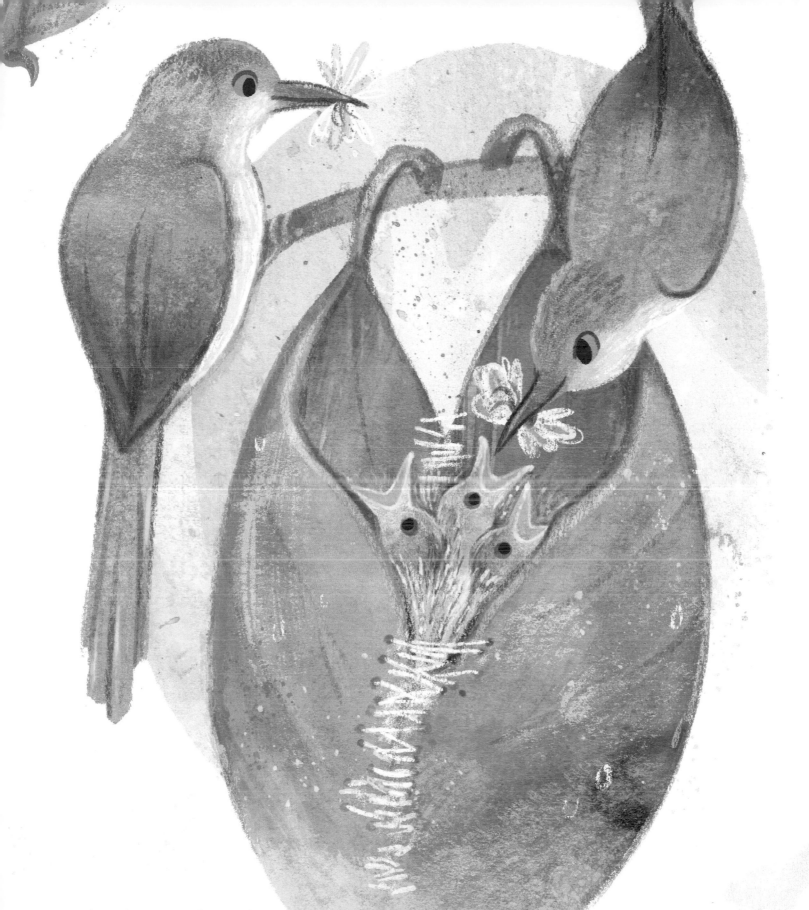

Tailorbirds use fibers from plants to sew leaves together, making a deep cup where they tuck away their nest, keeping it hidden from view.

This one spits water at bugs—
it's got great aim.

Archerfish spit jets of water at insects sitting on branches, knocking them into the water so the fish can gobble them up. They can hit targets up to six feet (two meters) away.

This animal breaks shells on its chest. (You might think that would hurt, but it doesn't seem to.)

A sea otter floats on its back in the ocean and breaks open sea urchins and clams by bashing them on a stone resting on its stomach.

This animal makes hooks for pulling out grubs.

New Caledonian crows make hooks from bent twigs or strips from pandanus palm leaves, which they use to pull beetle grubs out of holes in trees.

This animal uses sticks to catch birds—that's low.

In the nesting season, when birds like herons and egrets are busy collecting sticks to build their nests, a hungry mugger crocodile will balance some sticks on its head and swim close by, staying well hidden underwater. When a bird reaches out for one, the crocodile makes a grab for the bird.

And these ones drop tiny pebbles
down holes—look out below!

Pyramid ants and honey ants eat the same food. Pyramid ants drop
tiny stones and leaves down the nest holes of honey ants, which probably makes the
honey ants think they're being attacked. They rush about trying to defend
their nest instead of going out to feed, leaving more food for the pyramid ants.

This animal makes a bower for his
mate, using flowers and shells.

A male bowerbird makes a complicated shelter, called a bower, out of twigs and small sticks to attract a mate. He decorates it with flowers, shells, and brightly colored trash, spending hours arranging things until they look just right!

This animal throws stones at eggs.

Egyptian vultures crack open ostrich eggs by dropping pebbles on them.
Sometimes it takes a long time.

This one makes drumsticks instead.

To show off to his mate, a male palm cockatoo
will break a thick twig off a branch and use it
to beat the sides of their nest hole.

And this one uses cow dung as bait.
It really smells!

Burrowing owls carry pieces of dung from cows and other animals and drop them around the entrance of their nest burrow. The smell attracts dung beetles, which make a tasty snack for the owls.

Animals usually use just one tool, but some use quite a few:

sticks for digging up roots,

grass stems for fishing out termites,

and rocks to crack open nuts.

Chimpanzees use all these different tools. Young chimpanzees
learn how by copying their mothers and older relatives.

But the animal that uses
the most tools of all . . .

is you!

More About Animals and Tools

Many of the animals that use tools are ones that can pick things up quite easily with their hands and feet or claws and bills. Our clever fingers and thumbs help make humans champion tool users. We can make tools of all shapes and sizes, too.

Apart from humans, chimpanzees use more kinds of tools than any other animal. Other apes, like orangutans, and monkeys, like capuchins, baboons, and macaques, are also pretty good tool users. Most animal tools are used for getting food, but some animals also make tools to clean themselves, to use as sponges for holding water, or sometimes even to use as umbrellas!

INDEX